Arts and Crafts Fun

Fun Crafts
with
Colors

Enslow Elementary
an imprint of
Enslow Publishers, Inc.
40 Industrial Road   PO Box 38
Box 398   Aldershot
Berkeley Heights, NJ 07922 Hants GU12 6BP
USA   UK
http://www.enslow.com

Enslow Elementary, an imprint of Enslow Publishers, Inc.

Enslow Elementary® is a registered trademark of Enslow Publishers, Inc.

English edition copyright © 2006 by Enslow Publishers, Inc.

Translated from the Spanish edition by Toby S. McLellan, edited by Susana C. Schultz, of Strictly Spanish, LLC. Edited and produced by Enslow Publishers, Inc.

Library-in-Cataloging Publication Data

Ros, Jordina.
  [Colores. English]
  Fun crafts with colors / Jordina Ros, Pere Estadella.
    p.   cm. — (Arts and crafts fun)
  Originally published: Barcelona, Spain : Parramón, c2003.
  ISBN 0-7660-2655-8
  1. Art—Technique—Juvenile literature. 2. Color in art—Juvenile literature.
3. Handicraft—Juvenile literature. I. Estadella, Pere. II. Title. III. Series.
  N7440.R67313 2005
  701'.85—dc22
                    2005011219

Originally published in Spanish under the title *Los colores*.
Copyright © 2003 PARRAMÓN EDICIONES, S.A., - World Rights.
Published by Parramón Ediciones, S.A., Barcelona, Spain.
Spanish edition produced by: Parramón Ediciones, S.A.
Authors: Jordina Ros and Pere Estadella
Collection and scale model design: Comando gráfico, S.L.
Photography: Estudio Nos & Soto, Corel
© Willem de Kooning, VEGAP, Barcelona
Parramón Ediciones, S.A., would like to give special thanks to Pol, Eugenia, and Beatriz, who did such a wonderful job posing for the photographs in this book.

Printed in Spain

10 9 8 7 6 5 4 3 2 1

Fun Crafts with Colors

Table of Contents

Things to Remember . . .

Make sure you have everything you need!
Before you start the craft, go over the list of materials.

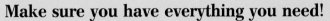

Be careful with sharp objects!
You may be using sharp tools, such as scissors or something to punch holes with. Always ask an adult for permission or for help!

Be careful when painting!
Protect your workspace with newspaper or plastic so that it does not get stained with paint. Clean the paintbrushes well so they don't get damaged. When you are finished painting, close the paint containers so the paint does not dry out.

Imagination
If you come up with a new idea while working on these crafts, tell a teacher or another adult. Together you can create new crafts that are all your own.

What Is Color All About?

Why does blue look different than purple? And why does dark blue look different than light blue? What is color all about?

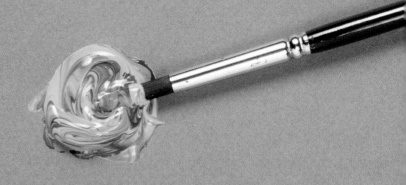

Look around you. People, animals, landscapes, and objects—they are all different colors. Look at a single flower, or even a leaf—is it really all just one color? How many different colors do you see in it?

Color and Emotion

You can express your emotions with color. What feelings do you associate with red? Yellow? Blue? How do you feel when you are looking at bright colors? Dark colors? Soft colors, like pastels?

How Does Paint Get Its Color?

You probably know that there are different types of paints—oil, watercolor, acrylic, and so on. Each has a different type of liquid for its base. The color comes from the pigment or dye that is mixed in with the base.

Many pigments and dyes come from things in nature, such as fruit, plants, or soil. You can even make a simple kind of paint called tempera by mixing colored pigment with an egg! Try making your own tempera by mixing an egg yolk with some red soil or the liquid you get from squeezing grass or blueberries.

Color and Light

We can see because our eyes sense light. And as light reflects off different surfaces in different ways, we see all the different colors. Colors also look brighter and stronger when the light is very bright. When there is less light, colors look softer or muted.

Close your eyes! Without them, you couldn't see anything. But did you know you also need light to see?

Look out your window at night. You will see shades of gray and black.

During the day, you can see all the different colors—green, blue, yellow, orange...

Have you ever noticed the sun shining while it was raining? If the sunlight reflects off the drops of water the right way, you will see a rainbow!

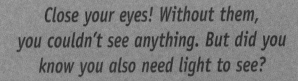
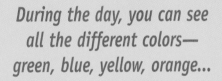

Looking at Colors

The three basic colors—red, blue, and yellow—are called **primary colors.**

You can make **secondary colors** by mixing primary colors together. Purple, orange, and green are secondary colors.

RED

BLUE

YELLOW

Try these mixtures. Use equal amounts of each color.

RED + BLUE = PURPLE

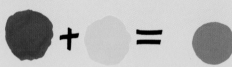

RED + YELLOW = ORANGE

YELLOW + BLUE = GREEN

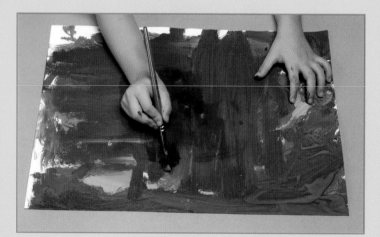

How We See Different Colors

Did you know that the light from the sun includes all the colors we can see? If you have ever seen sunlight shine through a prism, you know that it breaks up into all the colors of the rainbow! When light hits a surface, some of the light is absorbed. The rest is reflected off the surface. A red apple reflects the part of the light that our eyes see as red. A green apple reflects the part that we see as green.

You probably know that you can make black paint by mixing all the other colors together. And most people would probably think of white as being no color. But how do we see black and white? An object that looks black to us absorbs all of the light shining on it. It reflects back no color. Something that looks white to us absorbs none of the light shining on it. It reflects all of the colors together, as white. Isn't that interesting?

Color All Around Us

Look around—large and small patches of color are everywhere!

This soccer field is a big patch of green. It covers a large space.

This man is a small black patch against the orange sky.

This swimming pool is a medium-sized patch of blue.

Color is also used in signs and signals as a way of communicating. Colors are often used as symbols in art and writing to express certain ideas. We are surrounded by colors!

Signs and Signals

A special color may be used to communicate specific information. When you see it, you know what to do! The colors of a traffic signal tell us when to stop, when to slow down, and when to go. The different colors of street signs also help us to tell them apart. If you're seeing red, it's probably time to stop. And if you see green . . . *GO!*

Symbols

Different colors can also serve as symbols. A symbol is something that represents a certain idea. When you see it, you think of that idea.
- Red can mean love...or anger!
- Yellow might represent happiness.
- White often symbolizes peace or purity.
- Blue can also symbolize peace.
- Purple can mean royalty, nobility, or courage.
What other color symbols can you think of?

Three Little Hedgehogs

What you will need...

Fifteen flat toothpicks
Clay
Red, yellow, and blue poster paints
Sponge

For this craft, you will use the three primary colors—red, yellow, and blue!

While the paint is drying, you can mold the clay!

Stick fifteen flat toothpicks into a sponge. Paint five of them red, five of them yellow, and the other five blue.

Mold three medium balls of clay.

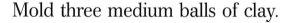

Before the clay dries, push the red toothpicks into one of the balls of clay, the blue toothpicks into another one, and the yellow toothpicks into the last one.

Now you will paint the balls of clay to match!

Paint the ball with the blue toothpicks blue, the one with the yellow toothpicks yellow, and the one with the red toothpicks red!

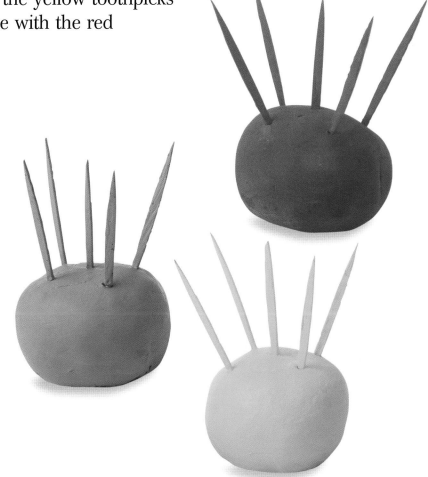

These are some pretty wild hedgehogs!

YOU CAN TRY
Try making three more hedgehogs using the secondary colors of purple, orange, and green. What a zoo!

White on Black, Black on White

What you will need...

White and black poster board
White and black shiny paper
Scissors
Glue stick
Ruler
White and black pencils

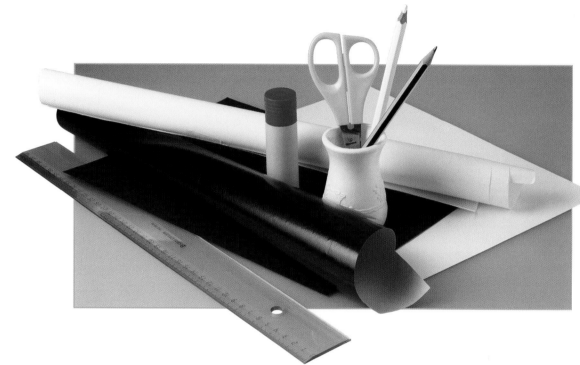

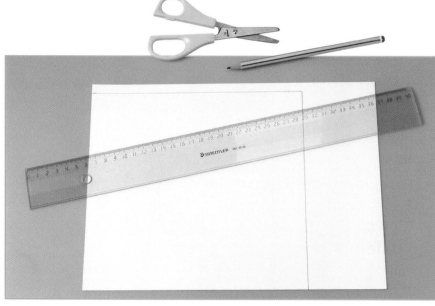

Use a pencil and ruler to draw
a 3-inch square on the white
poster board. Cut it out.

*For this craft you will be
using the ruler a lot!*

Draw a rectangle that is 3 inches long by 1-1/2 inches wide on the black poster board. Cut it out.

Glue the black rectangle onto the white square so that it covers one half of it.

You are going to mix white with black and black with white!

Tear five pieces of white shiny paper in different sizes.

Tear five pieces of black shiny paper in different sizes.

Now glue the white pieces onto the black half of your black and white square. Glue the pieces in order from biggest to smallest.

What a contrast!

Now glue the black pieces onto the white half of your square, in order from biggest to smallest.

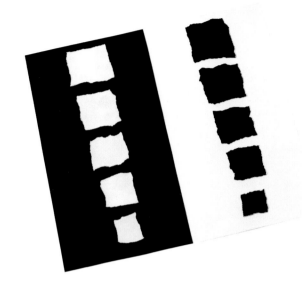

With white and black you can make amazing contrasts!

YOU CAN TRY
Try making other shapes with black and white construction paper. How would you make a zebra?

Fire and Water

What you will need...

Orange and blue poster board
Red, orange, yellow, pink, blue, and white poster paint
Red, orange, yellow, pink, blue, and white tissue paper
Tracing paper
Two cardboard toilet paper tubes
Scissors
Pencil
Hole puncher or scissors
Paintbrushes
Pattern (page 46)

Do you know the difference between
warm colors and cool colors? Can you guess?

Trace the fire pattern
(page 46) onto the
orange poster board.
Punch or cut it out
of the poster board.

Now trace the pattern of a drop of water (page 46) onto the blue poster board. Punch or cut it out of the poster board.

Fire burns and water cools, right?

Paint one of the tubes with warm colors. Try red, orange, yellow, and pink. This will be the fire tube.

And what about the other tube?

To make the water tube, paint it with cool colors. Try different shades of blue and white.

Glue the fire tube onto the orange base. Glue the water tube onto the blue base.

Tear the warm colored tissue paper into strips and crumple them. Place them in the fire tube.

Now you are going to make fire and water—with tissue paper!

Tear the cool colored tissue paper into strips and crumple them. Put them into the water tube.

Now you know which of these colors are warm and which ones are cool! What other colors might you think of as being warm or cool?

YOU CAN TRY

You can keep your water tubes near the kitchen or bathroom sink. Put the fire tube on the hot water side and the water tube on the cold water side. What else can you make with warm and cool colors?

Stamp It!

You can mix primary colors to make secondary colors.
Do you want to experiment?

Pour a little yellow and a little red paint in a container. Mix them with a paintbrush and you will have orange.

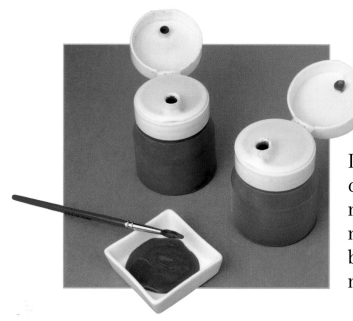

In another container, mix a little red and a little blue paint to make purple.

What about green?

To make green, mix a little blue paint with a little yellow.

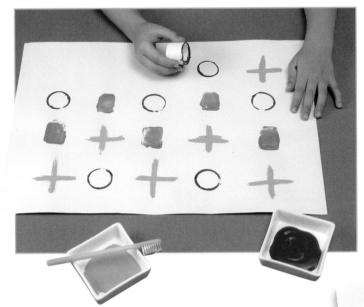

Use different objects as stamps—the toothbrush, the glue stick cap, and the eraser with the toothpick stuck into it as a handle. Dip each one into one of the paints you prepared. Stamp them several times on the white poster board until you have a fun combination of colors and shapes.

Now you have a great poster showing the secondary colors orange, purple, and green— but you used only the primary colors yellow, red, and blue!

YOU CAN TRY

Try making your own gift wrap by stamping a brown paper bag or tissue paper. Make some with the primary colors and some with secondary colors.

A Party of Materials

What you will need...

Rectangular wooden board
Pencil
White cloth
Newspaper
Sand
Green, yellow, and orange poster paints
Plastic container
Paintbrush
Glue stick
Plastic spoon
Roller

For this craft, you will mix different colors and materials. It will be fun!

In a container, mix sand and orange paint.

Use the plastic spoon to spread the orange sand onto the top third of the wooden board.

Now for the cloth...

Cut or tear the white cloth into small pieces. Glue them below the stripe of orange sand.

Paint the white cloth with green paint until the middle stripe is completely covered.

And the newspaper!

Tear a strip of newspaper. Make it about the same length and width as the bottom section of the board.

Crumple the paper a little, straighten it back out, and glue it onto the board.

Use the roller to paint the newspaper yellow.

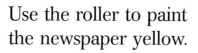

Was it fun to mix different colors and materials? How does each section look and feel different from the rest?

YOU CAN TRY

Look for other things you can paint to make new textures. Be sure to ask an adult first!

Natural Colors

What you will need...

Cherries or strawberries
Egg yolk
Chocolate or dark brown clay
Freshly cut grass
White poster board
Pencil
Paintbrush
Small plastic dish
Ruler

VERY IMPORTANT TIP!
Ask an adult for help with this craft. If you are allergic to any of the foods in this craft, please do not do it!

Do you want to know what natural pigments are?

Draw a horizontal line and a vertical line through the center of the poster board to divide it into four parts. Rub a cherry or strawberry on one part. You will get the color red!

Put an egg yolk in the dish and mix it up a little with the paintbrush. Paint it onto another part of the poster board. Now you have the color yellow.

Would you like to make the color green?

Rub some freshly cut grass onto another part of the poster board to make green.

Don't eat the chocolate— you'll need it to make great art!

Rub the last part of the poster board with a piece of chocolate to make brown. If you don't have chocolate on hand, you can also make this color with a little clay.

Natural pigments are colors that come from things you can find in nature.

(Of course you won't find chocolate bars in nature— but they are made with cacao beans, which are natural!)

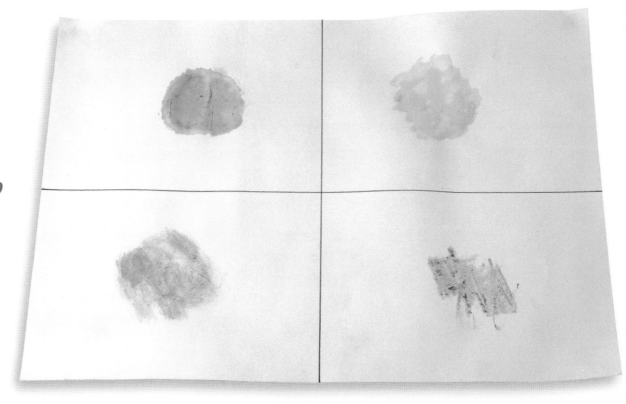

Little Colored Boxes

What you will need...

Eight small empty boxes (tops and bottoms)
Black poster board
White, pink, orange, green, and blue poster paints
Glue stick
Plastic egg cartons
Plastic spoons
Paintbrushes

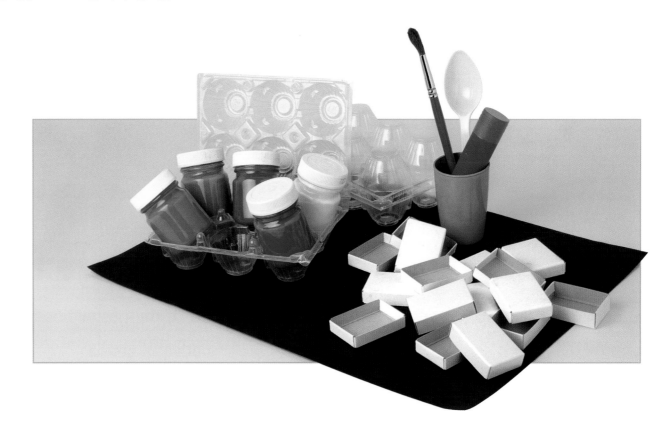

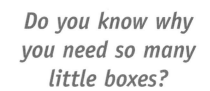

Do you know why you need so many little boxes?

You are going to make a poster that shows four different shades of four different colors!

Pour a little pink paint into four cups of an egg carton. Leave the first one unmixed. Add a little white paint to the second. Add a little more white paint to the third, and even more white paint to the fourth.

Each color will get lighter as you add white to it. This is how you make different shades!

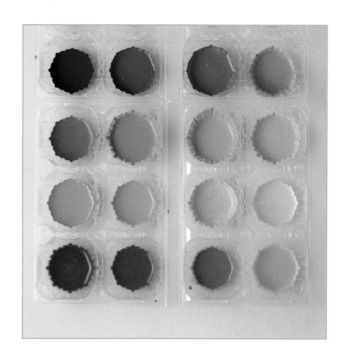

In the other cups of the egg carton, prepare different shades of green, orange, and blue.

Take four of your sixteen box tops or bottoms. Paint each one a different shade of pink.

Paint the rest of the little boxes with the other colors: four with shades of orange, four with shades of green, and four with shades of blue.

Be sure to let the paint dry on all the boxes!

Now arrange the boxes so the different shades of each color are in order from darkest to lightest.

Glue the boxes to the black poster board. Keep them in order from darkest to lightest.

Don't these different shades of color look striking on the black background? You can do this with any colors you like!

YOU CAN TRY
Choose your favorite poster paint color. What happens when you keep adding white paint? Try to make ten different shades of that color.

Pizza!

What you will need...
Large round plastic or paper plate
Red, green, orange, pink, and blue clay
Green, orange, pink, red, and blue finger paints

*Do you like combining colors? For this craft,
you will make an amazing pie of many colors!*

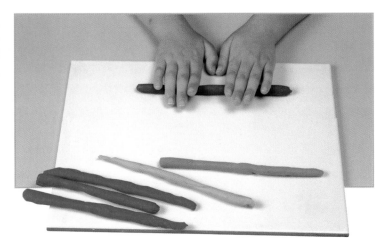

Make four sticks of red clay.
Then make one stick each of
green, blue, orange, and pink.

Cover the edges of the plate with the four
sticks of red clay. Add the other sticks so
they divide the plate into four parts.

Paint the part between the orange and green sticks with orange and green finger paints.

Do the same in the other three parts. Use green and pink paints between the green and pink clay sticks, pink and blue paints between the pink and blue sticks, and blue and orange paints between the blue and orange sticks.

What a crazy combination of colors! Are other combinations coming to mind?

TIP
You can use poster paints and a paintbrush instead of finger paints.

The Big Lake

What you will need...

Blue poster board
Blue metallic paper
Green corrugated cardboard
Green, yellow, and red round stickers
Hole puncher or scissors
Pencil
Glue stick
Pattern (page 47)

For this craft you will be making a big lake!

Glue the blue metallic paper to the poster board. The poster board should be totally covered.

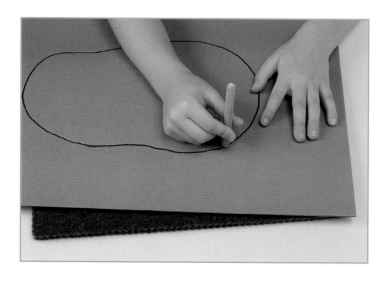

Trace the lake shape from the pattern (page 47) onto the back side of the green cardboard. Punch or cut out the shape.

Glue the green cardboard to the poster board. The rough side of the cardboard should be facing up.

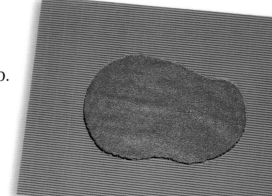

Add some colored stickers to the lake to make little fishes.

What a lovely blue lake in the middle of a green valley. Can you imagine swimming in it on a hot summer day?

TIP
If you can't find green corrugated cardboard, you can paint regular corrugated cardboard green. You can also use construction paper instead of the blue metallic paper and cardboard.

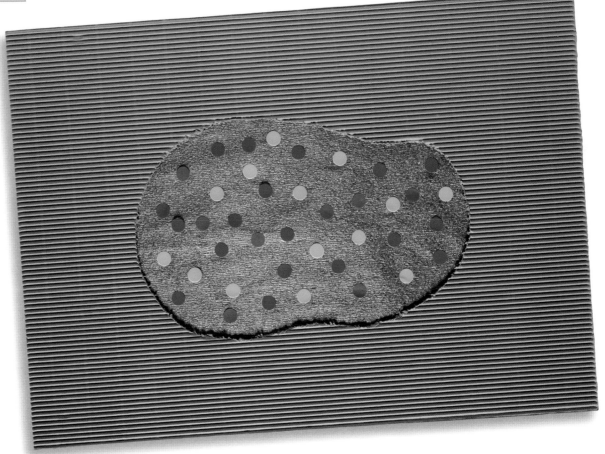

All the Same...but Different!

What you will need...
Three white poster boards
Black, blue, pink, and yellow poster paints
Colored yarn
Colored stickers
Colored chalks
Three rollers
Paintbrushes
Glue stick
Scissors

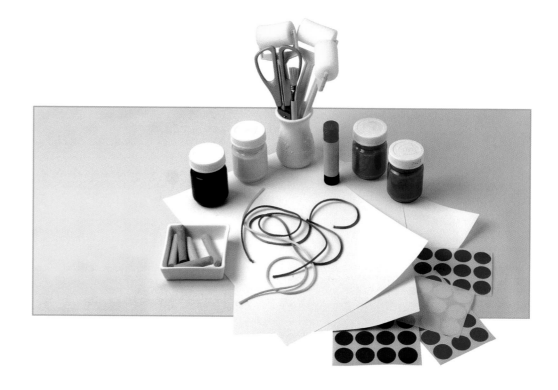

These three poster boards are all the same. Let's make them different!

Paint one of the white poster boards with black paint. Let it dry.

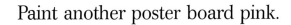
Paint another poster board pink.

And now paint the last poster board blue.

Make sure the paint is dry on all the poster boards before continuing!

Glue each of the poster boards along their short ends to make three cylinders.

Now to decorate the cylinders!

Paint green and yellow patches on the pink cylinder.

Cut six pieces of yarn, each long enough to go around a cylinder. Use different colored stickers to attach the yarn to the blue cylinder.

And what can you do with the black cylinder?

Color the black cylinder with colored chalk.

Place the three cylinders together. See how different they look, even though they have the same shape!

YOU CAN TRY
Try making cubes or boxes out of construction paper. How can you make them look different?

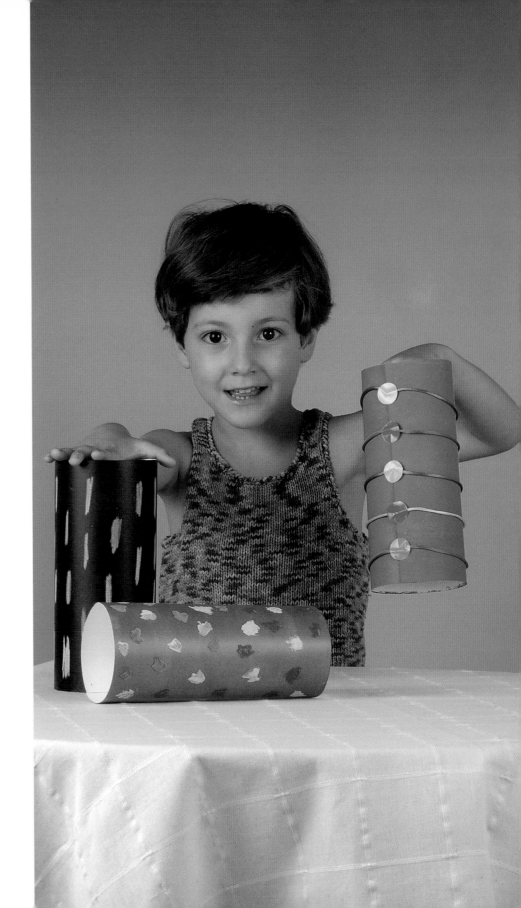

Fall and Spring

What you will need...
Photograph of a fall landscape from a magazine
Photograph of a spring landscape from a magazine
Two white poster boards
Poster paint (different colors)
Paint containers
Pieces of sponge
Glue stick

For this craft, you will look at the different colors of fall and spring.

Notice the main colors in the spring photograph. Use a sponge to stamp the same colors onto one of the white poster boards until it is completely covered.

And now...fall!

Find the main colors in the fall landscape. Stamp those colors onto the other white poster board until it is completely covered.

When the spring poster board is dry, glue your spring photograph to the center.

When the fall poster board is dry, glue your fall photograph to the center.

Wow! What a great way to show the colors of the seasons!

YOU CAN TRY
Try doing the same for winter and summer. What colors do you think you will need for those seasons?

Robot Eyes

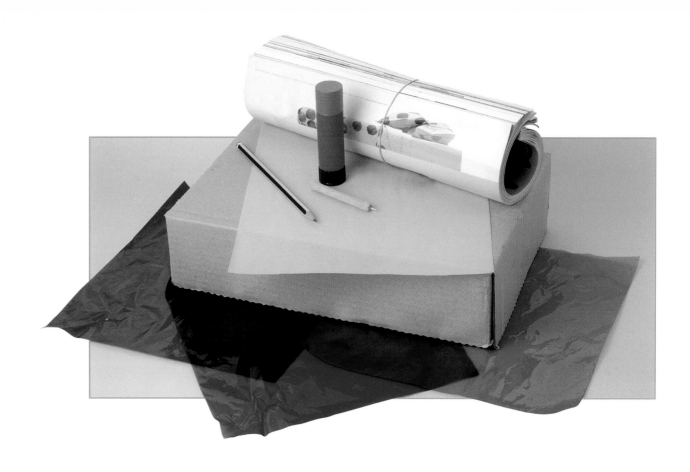

What you will need...
Top of a cardboard box
Red, blue, and orange cellophane
Magazines
Hole puncher or scissors
Pencil
Glue stick
Tracing paper
Pattern (page 48)

Can you imagine seeing everything in red or blue?

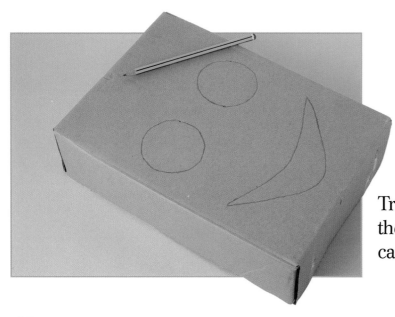

For this craft, you will be working with color using a transparent or see-through material—cellophane!

Trace the eyes and mouth from the pattern (page 48) onto the cardboard box.

Punch or cut out the
eyes and mouth.

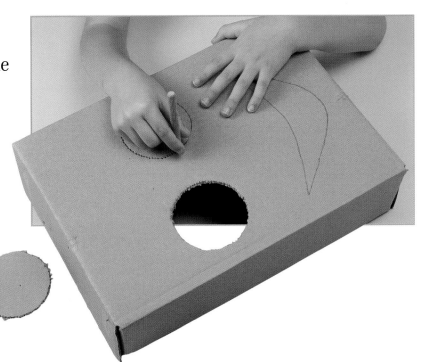

Tear pieces from the magazine pages so
that you have enough to cover the lid.

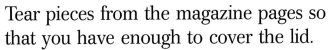

Glue the magazine pieces to the lid.
Don't cover the holes you made for
the eyes and mouth!

Now glue a piece of red cellophane behind one eye, a piece of blue behind the other eye, and a piece of orange behind the mouth.

Place the lid in front of you like a mask. Surprise! With one eye you can see everything in red, and with the other eye everything looks blue!

TIP
Be careful—do not walk around with your mask on!

"Red Man with Moustache" by Willem de Kooning (1904–1997)

The painter Willem de Kooning was born in Holland. He used patches of color in his paintings to create colorful effects.

Do you know the name he gave this painting? It is called *Red Man with Moustache*. You may find it difficult to see the person clearly. But you can imagine him!

Colors are everywhere. Imagine seeing things in different colors. Have fun with them!

Fire and Water

Pages 16–19

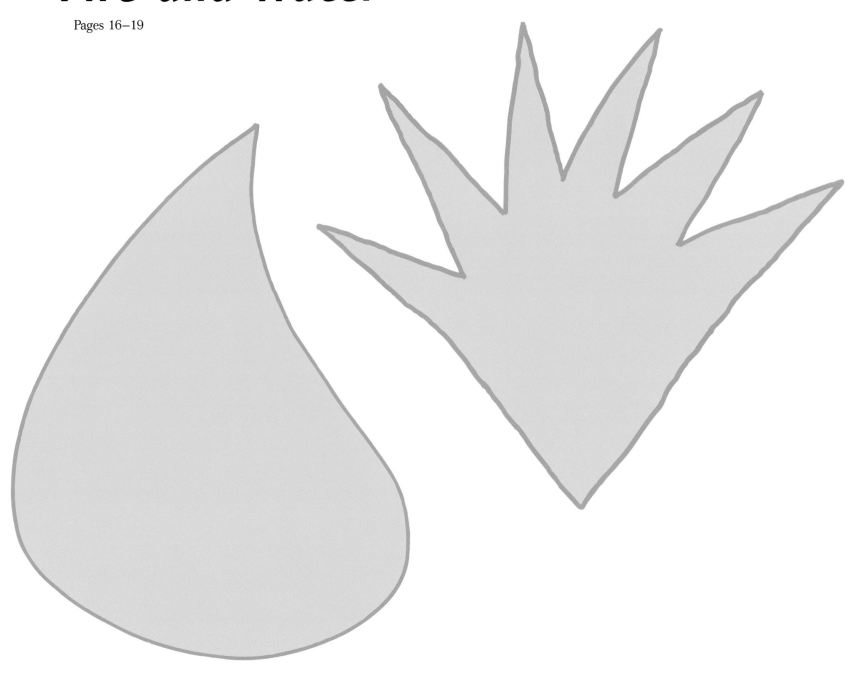

The Big Lake

Pages 34–35

Robot Eyes

Pages 42–44

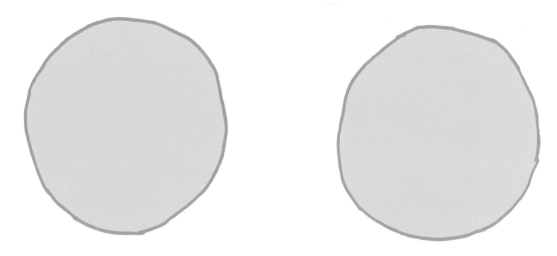